W9-CQY-301

**For Belinda, Bob, Anne
and everyone fighting to protect
these animals in their habitat**

*A percentage of the royalties from
this book is being donated to the
Wildlife Protection Society of India*

Copyright © 1999 Flora McDonnell
Dual Language Copyright © 1999
Mantra Publishing

First published 1999 by
Walker Books Ltd
This edition published 2002

Printed in Hong Kong

Published by
Mantra Publishing
5 Alexandra Grove
London N12 8NU
www.mantrapublishing.com

水花飛濺
Splash!

Flora McDonnell

Chinese translation by
Sylvia Denham

mantra

熱呀！熱呀！熱呀！
大笨象覺得很熱。

Hot, hot, hot!
The elephants
are hot.

老虎覺得很熱。

Tiger is hot.

犀牛覺得很熱。

Rhinoceros is hot.

讓我們跟著小象⋯

Let's follow the baby
down to the ...

下 水 去 。 眞 舒 暢 的 水 。

water. Lovely water.

水用來喝。
水用來…

Water to drink.
Water to ...

squirt,   噴呀，
squirt,   噴呀，
squirt!   噴呀！

Splash!
goes Mother Elephant.

水濺濕了
大象媽媽。

潑呀！
犀牛也被水淋濕。

Splosh! goes Rhinoceros.

Whoosh! Sploosh! goes Tiger.

噓呀！
潑呀！
老虎也濕啦。

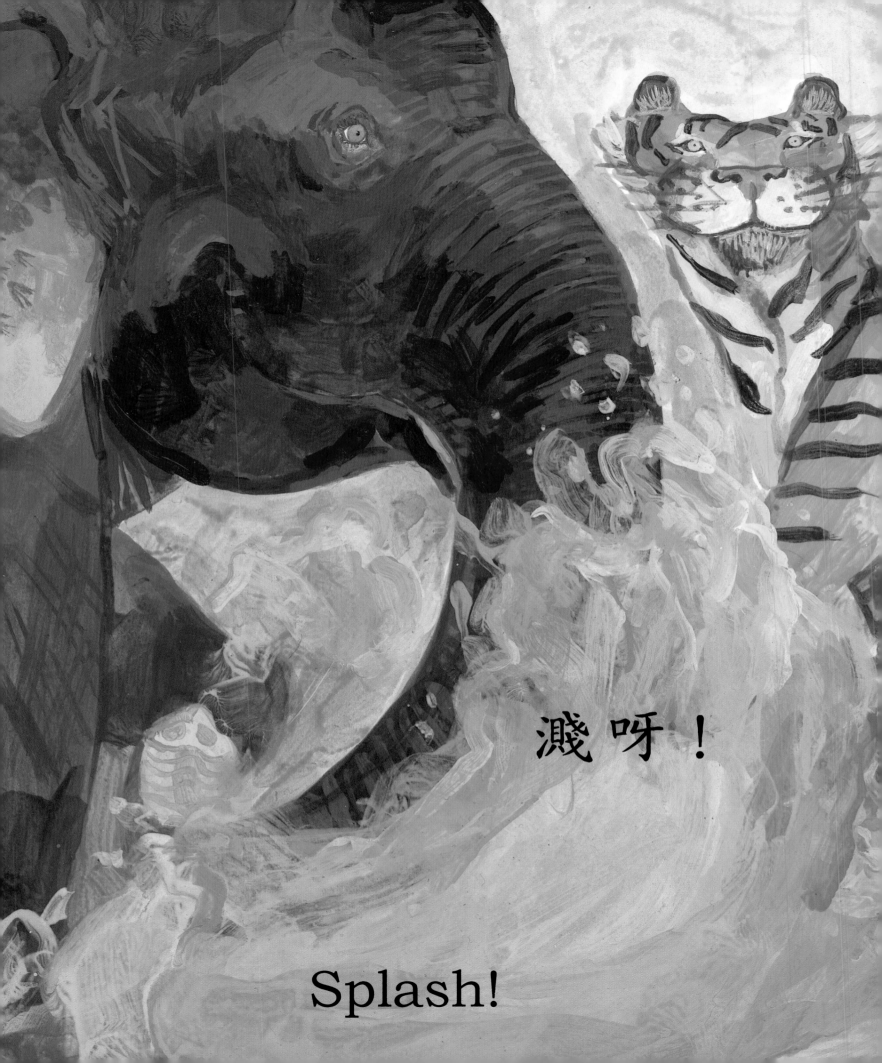

老虎現在又涼快又開心。

Now Tiger is cool
and happy.

犀牛現在又涼快又開心。

Now Rhinoceros is cool
and happy.

大象媽媽現
在又涼快又
開心。

Now Mother
Elephant is
cool and happy.

精靈的小象真
開心，真涼
快！

What a happy,
cool, clever little
baby elephant!